ADAM HAMILTON

Revival
Faith as Wesley Lived It

Children's Leader Guide

by Sally Hoelscher

Abingdon Press
Nashville

Revival: Faith as Wesley Lived It
Children's Leader Guide

This book is printed on acid-free, elemental chlorine-free paper.

ISBN 978-1-426-78871-0

14 15 16 17 18 19 20 21 22 23—10 9 8 7 6 5 4 3 2 1

MANUFACTURED IN THE UNITED STATES OF AMERICA

Contents

To the Leader

This children's leader guide is designed for use with Adam Hamilton's book and program *Revival: Faith as Wesley Lived It.* This guide includes six lessons that follow the life of John Wesley. Children will learn about John Wesley's life and ministry and will explore six characteristics that Wesley felt defined Christians.

The lessons in this guide, designed for children five to eleven years old, are presented in a large group/small group format. Children begin with time spent at activity centers, followed by time together as a large group. Children end the lesson in small groups determined by age. Each lesson plan contains the following sections:

Focus for the Teacher

The information in this section will provide you with background information about the week's lesson. Use this section for your own study as you prepare.

Explore Interest Groups

You'll find in this section ideas for a variety of activity centers. The activities will prepare the children to hear the Bible story. Allow the children to choose one or more of the activities that interest them. Occasionally there will be an activity that is recommended for all children, usually because it relates directly to a later activity. When this is the case, it will be noted in the sidebar notes.

Large Group

The children will come together as a large group to hear the story for the week. This section begins with a transition activity followed by the story and a Bible verse activity. A worship time concludes the large-group time.

Small Groups

Children are divided into age-level groups for small-group time. Depending on the size of your class, you may need to have more than one group for each age level. It is recommended that each small group contain no more than ten children.

Younger Children

The activities in this section are designed for children five to seven years old.

Older Children

The activities in this section are designed for children eight to eleven years old.

Reproducible Pages

At the end of each lesson are reproducible pages to be photocopied and handed out for all the children to use during that lesson's activities.

Schedule

Many churches have weeknight programs that include a meal, an intergenerational gathering, and classes for children, youth, and adults. This schedule illustrates one way to organize a weeknight program.

5:30	Meal
6:00	Intergenerational gathering introducing weekly themes and places for the lesson. This time may include presentations, skits, music, and opening or closing prayers.
6:15–8:15	Classes for children, youth, and adults.

Churches may want to do this study as a Sunday school program. The following schedule takes into account a shorter class time, which is the norm for Sunday morning programs.

10 minutes	Intergenerational gathering
45 minutes	Classes for children, youth, and adults

Choose a schedule that works best for your congregation and its Christian education programs.

Blessings to you and the children as you explore faith as Wesley lived it!

1 Prayer Always Talk to God

<table>
<tr><td>

Objectives

The children will
- hear what the Bible teaches about prayer.
- learn about John Wesley's early life.
- discover that John Wesley learned about prayer from his mother.
- explore the importance of prayer in their lives.

</td><td>

Theme

You can pray about anything.

Bible Verse

Pray continually. (1 Thessalonians 5:17)

</td></tr>
</table>

Focus for the Teacher

Welcome to *Revival!* In the eighteenth century, a man named John Wesley began a movement aimed at revitalizing Christianity in Britain. The societies begun by Wesley were the beginnings of the Methodist church that eventually spread across England, America, and the world.

Throughout this study, the children in your class will learn about John Wesley's life, where he lived, and ideas he felt were important to the Christian faith. The lessons are theme-based. Each week, children will hear not only John Wesley's connection to the theme, but also what the Bible teaches us about it.

We begin our study looking at John Wesley's early life and discussing prayer. John Wesley learned about prayer from his mother, Susanna, who was very influential in his life. Children may have the idea that prayer is something we do only at special times, such as mealtimes or bedtimes, or in special places, such as church. Help the children understand that prayer can happen anytime and anywhere. Encourage them to ask for God's guidance in their lives, whether it be asking God

> Take some time to think about your own prayer life.

to help them get along with their family and friends or thanking God for the beautiful bird they saw outside their window this morning.

Young children see God as their friend and easily embrace the idea of praying about anything. With encouragement, they easily pray for themselves and others. They may need reminding that God does not always answer yes to our prayers.

Older children may be starting to have questions about prayer. They may ask why someone who is sick may not get better even after they pray for God to heal that person. They may need help in understanding that God does not always answer prayers in the way we think they should be answered. Respond to the children's questions honestly, admitting that you do not have all the answers.

As you introduce the children in your class to John Wesley and talk with them about prayer, take some time to think about your own prayer life. As you prepare your lesson, say a prayer of thanks for each child in your class.

Explore Interest Groups

Be sure that adult leaders are waiting when the first child arrives. Greet and welcome the children. Get the children involved in an activity that interests them and introduces the theme for the day's activities.

John Wesley and Me

Note: Encourage every child in your class to participate in this activity, as it provides important background for this six-week study

- **Say:** During this study, we are going to be learning about a man named John Wesley.

- **Ask:** Have you heard of John Wesley before? If so, what do you know about him?

- **Say:** John Wesley is an important person in the history of the Christian church. He is considered the founder of Methodism. Let's learn some facts about John Wesley and compare his life to yours.

- Give each child a copy of Reproducible 1a.

- Go through the worksheet together, encouraging the children to discuss the similarities and differences between John Wesley's life and their own.

- Encourage each child to complete the worksheet as you go through it together.

Prepare

✓ Provide copies of **Reproducible 1a: John Wesley and Me**, found at the end of the lesson.

✓ Provide pencils.

Make Prayer Beads

- **Say:** Today we are talking about prayer.

- **Ask:** When do you usually pray?

- **Say:** We know that we can pray anytime, but sometimes we forget that. You are going to make a keychain to serve as a prayer reminder.

- Have each child cut a length of string approximately two feet long.

- Have each child fold the string in half and put approximately one inch of the folded end of the string through the keychain ring.

- Have each child reach through the loop formed by the folded end of the string and pull both of the free ends of the string through the loop to secure the string to the ring.

- Give each child a set of letter beads to spell the word *PRAY*.

- Encourage the children to string beads on both ends of the string, spelling the word *PRAY* on one of the strings. Invite them to choose colors they enjoy.

- When they reach the end of the string or are done beading, have each child tie the two ends of the string together.

Prepare

✓ Provide beading string, keychain rings, scissors, plastic beads, and the following letter beads: P, R, A, Y.

- **Say:** When you take your keychain home, attach it to your backpack or use it as a zipper pull on your jacket. Every time you see it, let it remind you to say a prayer.

Praying with Crayons

- **Say:** There are many ways to pray. Some people like to pray while drawing.

- Give each child a piece of paper.

- Have each child use a crayon or marker to draw a free-form line on the paper that crosses over itself several times to create multiple spaces.

- Invite each child to write one person or thing they pray for in each of the spaces created by the line.

- Invite the children to use crayons or markers to decorate each space, thinking about what is written in the space as they are decorating it.

- **Say:** This is one way to pray.

Prepare

✓ Have available a CD player and a CD of upbeat Christian children's music.

✓ Inflate several balloons. The number of balloons to inflate will depend on the size of your class. Plan on one balloon for every ten children.

✓ Identify a large open area, free of obstacles, in which to play this game.

Prayer Volleyball

- **Say:** Today we are talking about prayer. One thing we know about prayer is that it is okay to pray anytime. Right now we are going to play a game and pray.

- Show the children the balloons.

- **Say:** Your challenge is to work together to keep the balloons in the air while the music plays. When the music stops, stay where you are and let the balloons fall to the ground.

- Play music and encourage the children to keep the balloons in the air.

- Stop the music.

- **Say:** Each time the music stops, I will shout out a prayer topic. Say a silent prayer for the people or situation mentioned. When the music starts up again, put the balloons back in the air.

- Shout out a category of something to pray for, such as family, friends, people in your school, children who go to bed hungry, people who live in a country at war, people who are sick, and so forth.

- Allow a few moments for silent prayer.

- Start the music again and encourage the children to keep the balloons aloft.

- Continue the game in this manner for four or five rounds, or until the children's energy begins to lag

Large Group

Bring all the children together to experience the Bible story. Use a bell to alert the children to the large-group time.

Where Is John?

- **Say:** For the next six weeks we will be learning about John Wesley. We will learn about different places that John lived. John Wesley was born in Epworth, a town in England. I have hidden a picture of John Wesley and the letters of the word *Epworth* around the room.

- Encourage the children to find the picture and letters.

- Have the children work together to put the letters in the correct order to spell *Epworth*.

- Show the children the world map or globe.

- **Ask:** Where do we live?

- Have the children identify where you are on the map or on the globe.

- **Say:** John Wesley lived in England, sometimes referred to as Great Britain.

- Have the children find England on the map or globe.

- Give each child a copy of the reproducible map.

- **Say:** This is a map of England.

- Have the children find Epworth on their maps.

- Collect the maps to be used next week.

Prepare

- ✓ Make one copy of **Reproducible 1b: John Wesley**, found at the end of the lesson. Cut out this picture of John Wesley and mount it on cardboard to make it sturdier. The picture will be used every week.

- ✓ Copy **Reproducible 1c: John Wesley's England**, found at the end of the lesson. Provide a copy of this map for each child.

- ✓ Write each of the following letters on a separate index card: E-P-W-O-R-T-H.

- ✓ Hide the picture of John Wesley and the index cards around the room.

- ✓ Have a world map or a globe available.

Prayer: Always Talk to God

- **Say:** For the next six weeks we are going to be learning about John Wesley.

- **Ask:** What have we learned about John Wesley so far today?

- Encourage the children to review what they have learned.

- Give each child a copy of Reproducible 1d.

- Invite a confident reader to read aloud the two sentences about prayer at the top of the page.

- Invite another confident reader to help you read the section titled "What Does the Bible Say About Prayer?" Have your volunteer read the regular print while you read the italicized Bible verses.

Prepare

- ✓ Provide each child with a copy of **Reproducible 1d: Prayer: Always Talk to God**, found at the end of the lesson.

- Invite a third reader to read the section "John Wesley and Prayer."
- **Ask:** Who taught John Wesley about prayer? Who teaches you about prayer?
- **Say:** John learned from his mother that prayer was important.

Prepare

✓ Write this week's Bible verse ("Pray continually." 1 Thessalonians 5:17) on a markerboard or piece of mural paper and place it where it can easily be seen.

In Other Words

- Show the children the Bible verse.
- **Say:** Our Bible verse today will be easy to remember because it is only two words!
- Invite the children to read the verse with you.
- **Ask:** What does the word *continually* mean? (Always or all the time)
- **Say:** Let's think of as many different ways to say "Pray continually" as we can.
- Encourage the children to come up with different ways to say the verse, such as "Pray all the time" or "Talk to God always."
- **Ask:** Is there any time when we can't pray? (No)

Many Ways to Pray

- **Say:** We often think of folding our hands together and bowing our heads when we pray. That's okay, but there are many other prayer positions. In fact, there's no wrong way to pray. Right now we are going to pray in several different ways. I will begin by saying a prayer position. Once everyone is in that position, I will say a short prayer. We will repeat that process several times.
- Lead the children in prayer, giving the following prayer positions and the corresponding prayers.

  o *Head bowed and hands folded*: God, we thank you that we can pray to you about anything.
  o *Hands raised high in the air*: God, we thank you that we can pray when we are joyful and excited.
  o *Shoulders slumped, face sad*: God, we thank you that you hear our prayers when we are sad.
  o *Kneeling*: God, help us to remember to talk with you often.
  o *Sports huddle*: God, we thank you that we can pray to you wherever we are.
  o *Standing, hands spread out to the side*: God, we thank you that we can pray to you about everything!
  o *Sitting*: God, we thank you for hearing our prayers. Amen.

- Dismiss children to their small groups.

Small Groups

Divide the children into small groups. You may organize the groups around age levels or around readers and nonreaders. Keep the groups small, with a maximum of ten children in each group. You may need to have more than one group of each age level.

Young Children (Ages 5-7)

- Have the children sit in a circle. Place the basket in the middle of the circle.
- **Say:** Let's review what we've learned today about John Wesley.
- Encourage the children to share what they remember, asking questions to assist them if necessary.
- **Say:** We have talked about prayer a lot today. John learned about the importance of prayer from his mother. The Bible tells us to pray all the time. I have some discussion questions for us about prayer.
- Invite a child to pick a card from the basket.
- Discuss the question on the chosen card as a class.
- Continue until all the questions have been discussed.
- **Say:** We can pray anytime and anywhere and about anything. Prayers don't need to be long. We can thank God for a beautiful sunset or ask God to be with people who might be hurt whenever we hear a siren. Even though we can pray in many ways, we sometimes forget to pray. Today we are going to make some prayer reminders.
- Give each child several index cards.
- Have each child write the word *PRAY* in large letters on each card. You may need to help the youngest children with the writing.
- Encourage the children to decorate their cards.
- **Say:** When you take these cards home, put them around your house in places where you will see them frequently. When you see a card, take a moment and say a prayer. The prayer doesn't need to be long or complicated. It can be as simple as "God, thank you for this day." Remember we can pray about anything!
- Invite children to share their joys and concerns for prayer time.
- **Pray:** Awesome God, thank you for hearing our prayers, even those we don't speak out loud. Today we pray for the joys and concerns we have mentioned. We thank you for John Wesley and for (*name each child in the small group*). Amen.

Prepare

✓ Provide index cards and markers.

✓ Write each of the following questions on an index card, emphasizing the first word by writing it in large letters and underlining it: Who do you pray for? What do you pray about? Where do you pray? When do you pray? Why do you pray? How do you pray?

✓ Place the index cards in a basket.

Prepare

✓ Provide paper, pencils, and a die.

✓ Tip: If you do not have a die, write the numbers 1 through 6 on separate small pieces of paper. Place the papers facedown in front of you and choose one of the papers to select a number.

Older Children (Ages 8–11)

- Have the children sit in a circle.

- **Ask:** What have you learned today about John Wesley?

- Allow the children an opportunity to share, asking questions to prompt them as needed.

- **Say:** John Wesley learned the importance of prayer from his mother.

- **Ask:** Do you feel comfortable praying in front of other people?

- **Say:** We know that prayer is important, and we know we can pray anytime, anywhere, and about anything; but praying with other people can sometimes make us uncomfortable. Maybe we worry that our prayers aren't good enough. Maybe we forget that prayers can be simple. Maybe we just need more practice! Today we are going to work together to write some prayers.

- Give each child a piece of paper and a pencil.

- Have each child write her or his favorite name for God at the top of the paper.

- Roll the die. Have the children pass their papers to the left that many times. For example, if you roll a three, all the papers will be handed left around the circle three times.

- Read the following directions, each time allowing the children time to write before rolling the die again and having the children pass their papers as above.

    o Write "Thank you, God, for . . ." and complete the sentence.
    o Write "Also thank you for . . ." and complete the sentence.
    o Write "Be with those who . . ." and complete the sentence.
    o Write "Help me to . . ." and complete the sentence.
    o Write "Amen."
    o Roll the die and have the children pass their papers one more time after "Amen."

- **Say:** For our closing prayer today, we will take turns reading our prayers aloud.

- Have the children take turns reading the prayers aloud.

- Encourage each child to take one of the prayers home.

John Wesley and Me

John Wesley is considered the founder of the Methodist church. Read the facts below about John Wesley's life. For each item, compare John's life with your own. Is it the same or different? In each box, write how John Wesley's life was the same or different from yours.

John Wesley was born on June 17, 1703.

John was born in England in a town called Epworth.

John's father, Samuel, was a pastor.

John's mother was named Susanna.

John's mother taught John, his brothers, and his sisters at home.

John had lots of brothers and sisters.

John Wesley

John Wesley's England

SCOTLAND

IRELAND

ENGLAND

WALES

• Epworth

Oxford
•

London
◉

Bristol
•

Prayer: Always Talk to God

Prayer is talking with God. We can pray anytime, anywhere, and about anything.

What does the Bible say about prayer?

Jesus prayed.
News of him spread even more and huge crowds gathered to listen and to be healed from their illnesses. But Jesus would withdraw to deserted places for prayer. (Luke 5:15-16)

Prayer played an important part in the lives of early Christians.
The believers devoted themselves to . . . their shared meals, and to their prayers. (Acts 2:42)

Pray all the time.
Rejoice always. Pray continually. Give thanks in every situation because this is God's will for you in Christ Jesus. (1 Thessalonians 5:16-18)
Offer prayers and petitions in the Spirit all the time. (Ephesians 6:18)

Pray instead of worrying.
Don't be anxious about anything; rather, bring up all of your requests to God in your prayers and petitions, along with giving thanks. (Philippians 4:6)

Pray for everyone, even people you don't like.
First of all, then, I ask that requests, prayers, petitions, and thanksgiving be made for all people. (1 Timothy 2:1)
But I say to you, love your enemies and pray for those who harass you so that you will be acting as children of your Father who is in heaven. (Matthew 5:44-45)

John Wesley and Prayer

John Wesley learned about prayer from his mother, Susanna. John's mother held family devotions in the kitchen every Sunday evening. She prayed for her children every day and spent an hour a week with each of them asking about their faith.

2 Holiness Do Everything for God

Objectives

The children will
- hear what the Bible teaches about holiness.
- learn about John Wesley's time at school.
- discover that John Wesley decided to give his whole life to God.
- explore the importance of holiness in their lives.

Theme

- Being holy means living the way God wants us to live.

Bible Verse

So, whether you eat or drink or whatever you do, you should do it all for God's glory. (1 Corinthians 10:31)

Focus for the Teacher

John Wesley's father was a preacher. His mother often led Bible studies. During John's early years, faith surely played an important role in his life. Then at the age of ten John went away to school in London. John himself later admitted that during this time he became negligent in his faith. It wasn't until John was older that he came to the decision to dedicate all of his life to God. John was determined to be what he referred to as an "altogether Christian"—doing everything to the glory of God.

> The Bible contains many words of wisdom and lessons.

We often present the Bible to children as a collection of stories. There is certainly truth in that representation; the Bible contains wonderful stories about fascinating people. However, the Bible is more than just stories.

The Scripture lessons in this study are not the typical Bible stories that we teach children. The Bible contains many words of wisdom and valuable lessons for life that are not in story form. The Bible can help us discover what God wants us to do and be.

The concept of being holy all the time or doing everything to the glory of God may be challenging for children to understand. As you discuss holiness with the children in your class, help them understand that being holy means always living in a way that God wants us to live. And how do we know how God wants us to live? By the example of Jesus, who not only taught us but showed us how to live.

Explore Interest Groups

Be sure that adult leaders are waiting when the first child arrives. Greet and welcome the children. Get the children involved in an activity that interests them and introduces the theme for the day's activities.

Holiness Scramble

- Have the children line up with their backs facing you.
- Place one sticky note on each child's back.
- **Say:** You each have a letter on your back. When I tell you to begin, you will need to work together to put yourselves in the correct order to spell "Holiness."
- Tell the children to begin.
- Encourage the children to work together.
- Check to see if the children are in the right order.
- **Ask**: What is holiness? What does it mean to be holy?
- **Say**: We are going to talk more about holiness during our large-group time.

Prepare

- ✓ Write the following word on sticky notes, one letter per sheet: *Holiness*.
- ✓ Tip: If you have a large class, divide the children into groups of eight for this activity.

Make a Clay Cross

- Divide the class into groups of eight children each.
- Give each group a bowl and a spoon.
- Have each group make a batch of air-drying clay by mixing together 1/4 cup each of flour, salt, cornstarch, and warm water. Add more water if the clay is too dry. If the clay is too wet, add more flour.
- Once the groups have made their clay, have them divide the clay into eight pieces, giving one piece to each group member.
- Give each child a piece of waxed paper to work on.
- Have children use their clay to make crosses.
- Give each child the option of using a toothpick to make a hole in the cross so it may be made into a necklace when dry.
- Invite the children to use watercolor paints to decorate their crosses.
- **Say:** This clay will be hard when it air-dries. If you have put a hole in your cross, you can make it into a necklace or an ornament. If you did not put a hole in your cross, you can set it on a shelf or table.
- **Ask:** What do you think of when you see a cross?
- **Say:** A cross can help us remember God and remind us to live the way Jesus taught us to live.

Prepare

- ✓ Provide flour, salt, cornstarch, water, bowls, spoons, measuring cups, toothpicks, waxed paper, watercolor paints, paintbrushes, plastic containers for water, and plastic table coverings or newspaper.
- ✓ Protect the work area with plastic table coverings or newspaper.
- ✓ Fill plastic containers one-third full with water and place them in the center of the table with the watercolor paints.
- ✓ Tip: If your time is limited, you may choose to make the clay before class.

Prepare

✓ Provide copies of **Reproducible 2a: John Goes to School**, found at the end of the lesson.

✓ Provide pencils.

Prepare

✓ Provide paper plates.

Learn More About John Wesley

- **Say:** Today we are continuing to learn about John Wesley.

- Give each child a copy of Reproducible 2a and a pencil.

- Encourage the children to decode the names of the schools John Wesley attended. (Answers: Charterhouse School, Christ Church, Lincoln College)

Plate Walk

- Divide the children into two groups.

- Have the groups stand in two lines, facing one another, about four feet apart.

- Give one child a paper plate and have him or her place it on his or her head.

- Have the child with the paper plate walk between the two lines of children.

- Have the lines of children try to make the plate fall by blowing or waving their hands. They may not touch the person, touch the plate, or move closer.

- Give each child an opportunity to walk through the line with a plate on her or his head.

- **Ask:** What did it feel like when you were walking through the line and everyone was trying to knock off the plate? Did it feel like you were all alone?

- **Say:** Sometimes peer pressure can be like this game. It feels like you are the only one with a plate on your head, and everyone else in the group is trying to knock it off! It takes courage to be different. Sometimes living as God wants us to live makes us feel like we are different from everyone else.

- Choose a child to walk through the line again. This time, let the child choose four friends to walk through the line with him or her. The friends will not have plates on their heads but may surround the plate-bearer and may use their hands to protect the plate. The friends may also say encouraging words.

- **Ask:** How was it different walking through the line with your friends helping you?

- **Say:** Our friends can help us and encourage us. It's important that we choose friends who will support us.

Large Group

Bring all the children together to experience the Bible story. Use a bell to alert the children to the large-group time.

Where Is John?

- **Say:** We are continuing to learn about John Wesley. Remember that John lived in England.
- Give each child a copy of the map.
- **Ask:** Where was John born? (Epworth)
- Have the children find Epworth on their maps.
- **Say:** I have hidden a picture of John Wesley and some letters around the room. The letters spell the name of the town where John went to college.
- Encourage the children to find the picture and letters.
- Have the children work together to put the letters in the correct order to spell *Oxford*.
- **Ask:** Where did John attend college? (Oxford)
- Have the children find Oxford on the maps.
- Collect the maps to be used next week.

Prepare

- ✓ Use the picture of John Wesley (Reproducible 1b) copied last week.
- ✓ Provide a copy of the map (Reproducible 1c) for each child.
- ✓ Write each of the following letters on a separate index card: O-X-F-O-R-D.
- ✓ Hide the picture of John Wesley and the index cards around the room.

Holiness: Do Everything for God

- **Say:** Let's review what we learned about John Wesley last week.
- Encourage children to share what they remember.
- **Say:** We just learned that John went to college in Oxford, England.
- Give each child a copy of Reproducible 2b.
- **Say:** Today we are going to read our story in a mixed-up way. We're going to read the last section first.
- Read or invite a confident reader to read aloud the section on "John Wesley and Holiness."
- **Ask:** What do you think John Wesley meant when he referred to himself as only "half a Christian"?
- Read the sentence about holiness at the top of the reproducible.
- Invite confident readers to read aloud the section called "What Does the Bible Say About Holiness?"
- **Ask:** What does it mean to do everything for the glory of God? What would it look like to glorify God when you are eating? (Perhaps saying a prayer of thanks for your food. Perhaps sharing your food with someone who is hungry.)
- **Say:** Being holy in all parts of our lives means always following God and living as Jesus taught us to live.

Prepare

- ✓ Make copies of **Reproducible 2b: Holiness: Do Everything for God**, found at the end of the lesson.

- **Ask:** What does following God and being holy look like when you are at school? at home? at the mall? at a sports event?
- Allow children an opportunity to share their ideas.
- **Say:** John Wesley realized that it is important to do everything for God, not just a few things, and to do so all the time, not just when it is convenient.

Prepare

✓ Write this week's Bible verse ("So, whether you eat or drink or whatever you do, you should do it all for God's glory." 1 Corinthians 10:31) on a markerboard or a piece of mural paper and place it where it can easily be seen.

Adjust the Volume of the Bible Verse

- Show the children the Bible verse.
- Encourage the children to read the Bible verse with you.
- **Say:** This verse sums up what we've been talking about today. Our goal is to live our entire life following God. Now let's pretend that I am a volume control slider. We will say the verse together three more times. When I am standing over here (move all the way to your right side) the volume needs to be very soft. As I walk across the room, the volume increases, and when I am standing over here (move all the way to your left side) the volume is very loud.
- Encourage the children to say the verse with you three more times as you control the volume with your position.

We Choose Holiness

- **Say:** Being holy means making God a priority in life, deciding to put God first. We are going to join together in a litany. Your response will be: "We choose holiness. We will put God first!"
- Have the children practice their response.
- Lead the children in the following litany, encouraging them to respond enthusiastically.

  o **Leader:** When we wake up in the morning we have a choice to make. Will we grumble that it's too early to get up, or will we thank God for the day?
  o **All:** We choose holiness. We will put God first!
  o **Leader:** The choices continue throughout the day. Will we always demand our own way, or will we consider the needs of others?
  o **All:** We choose holiness. We will put God first!
  o **Leader:** Will we say something mean, or will we choose kind words?
  o **All:** We choose holiness. We will put God first!
  o **Leader:** If we see someone in need, will we walk on by, or will we ask if we can help?
  o **All:** We choose holiness. We will put God first!
  o **Leader:** We remember that Jesus taught us to honor God and to love and serve others.
  o **All:** We choose holiness. We will put God first!
  o **Leader:** Amen.

- Dismiss children to their small groups.

Small Groups

Divide the children into small groups. You may organize the groups around age levels or around readers and nonreaders. Keep the groups small, with a maximum of ten children in each group. You may need to have more than one group of each age level.

Young Children (Ages 5-7)

- Have the children sit in a circle.

- **Say:** It's easy to say that we will choose to be holy and put God first, but it's not always easy to do. Let's spend some time thinking about what it means to be holy.

- **Ask:** Where is a place that you spend time? What do you think it means to put God first when you are at this place? What makes it hard to live like God wants you to when you are at this place?

- Allow the children to name places where they spend time, discussing each place by using the above questions.

- **Say:** John Wesley had a group of friends he saw often, kind of like our group of friends here. John and his friends encouraged each other to be holy and reminded each other what it meant to put God first in everything. We can encourage each other, too.

- Give each child an index card and a marker.

- Have each child write her or his name on the index card. You may need to help out the youngest children.

- Have the children pass their index cards to the person sitting on their right.

- Invite the children to write their names on the index cards they now have.

- Continue passing the cards and writing names until every card has everyone's name on it.

- **Say:** Take this card home with you. When you see it, remember that you have a group of friends who care about you. Let the card remind you that we are all trying to be holy in whatever we do.

- **Pray:** God, thank you for this time to be together and learn more about you. Help us remember to put you first and honor you in every part of our lives. Amen.

Prepare
- ✓ Provide index cards and markers.

Prepare

✓ Provide paper and pencils.

Older Children (Ages 8-11)

- Have the children sit in a circle.

- Give each child a piece of paper and a pencil.

- Have each child pick a day of the week and make a list of everything he or she does on that day, from waking up in the morning to going to sleep at night.

- Have the children talk together to help each other think of everything they do in a day.

- **Say:** Today we've been talking about holiness. Our Bible verse for the day says that we are to be holy in whatever we do. It's easy to say that we will put God first all the time, but it's not as easy to do.

- Have each child choose one thing on her or his list for the group to discuss. For each item shared, ask the following questions.

- **Ask:** What do you think it means to be holy when you are doing this activity? What would it look like to honor God and put God first during this activity? What makes it hard to be holy?

- Encourage children to offer their ideas and suggestions.

- If time permits, let each child share a second item from the list for discussion.

- **Say:** John Wesley had a group of friends that he saw often. John and his friends encouraged each other to be holy and reminded each other what it meant to put God first in everything they did.

- **Ask:** How can friends help you be holy?

- Have the children turn over their papers and write the names of three friends they can count on to help them remember to put God first.

- **Say:** This week, do your best to honor God and live as Jesus showed us how to live.

- **Pray:** God, thank you for friends who encourage us. Help us to be holy as you are holy. In everything we do, help us to put you first. Amen.

John Goes to School

Use the following key to decode the names of the schools John attended.

1 = U
2 = T
3 = S
4 = R
5 = O
6 = N
7 = L
8 = I
9 = H
10 = G
11 = E
12 = C
13 = A

John Wesley's early education took place at home. Susanna Wesley, John's mother, used the Bible to teach all her children how to read. When John was ten years old, he was sent to the following school in London.

12-9-13-4-2-11-4-9-5-1-3-11   3-12-9-5-5-7 _____

_____

When John was seventeen, he was ready to attend university. He began his studies at the following college at Oxford University.

12-9-4-8-3-2   12-9-1-4-12-9 _____

While at Oxford University, John became an ordained priest. He also began teaching at the following school.

7-8-6-12-5-7-6   12-5-7-7-11-10-11 _____

Holiness:
Do Everything for God

Being holy is being completely devoted to God and to doing God's work.

What Does the Bible Say About Holiness?

The Book of First Peter is a letter that one of Jesus' disciples wrote. In the letter, Peter encouraged people to follow Jesus' teachings. Peter also said, "Be holy in every aspect of your lives, just as the one who called you is holy" (1:15). Peter knew that if a person is truly following Jesus, that will show in every part of that person's life.

Paul, another follower of Jesus, wrote similar words in a letter to early Christians in Corinth. Paul said that everything should be done for God's glory—eating and drinking and everything else.

Being a Christian isn't a part-time job. Every moment of every day, Christians try to live as God wants us to live.

(Based on 1 Peter 1:13-16 and 1 Corinthians 10:31.)

John Wesley and Holiness

At the age of seventeen, John Wesley went to college in Oxford, England. John went on to become an ordained priest and a teacher at a college in Oxford. During his time at college, John realized that he was only "half a Christian." Throughout the rest of his life, John was determined to be what he called an "altogether Christian."

John knew it was important to try to be holy in all parts of his life. During his time at Oxford, John began to meet regularly with his brother Charles and a few other friends. In their time together, they encouraged each other and helped each other stay on track as they tried to be holy.

3 Faith Trust in God's Love

Objectives

The children will
- hear what the Bible teaches about faith.
- learn about John Wesley's experiences in Georgia and at Aldersgate.
- discover that John Wesley had questions about faith.
- explore their faith.

Theme

Through faith we can trust in God's never-ending love.

Bible Verse

God's faithful love lasts forever!
(Psalm 136:1b)

Focus for the Teacher

Knowing that John Wesley started a movement that grew and became Methodism, one might think he was a wildly successful preacher who inspired everyone he met. While John's passionate preaching did inspire many, he was also human. Like each of us, John Wesley experienced rejection. At times his spiritual and pastoral failures made him consider giving up preaching. It was during one of these times of failure and doubt that John experienced an "Aha!" moment that made him reconsider his understanding of faith.

After his time at Oxford University, John traveled to the American colony of Georgia to spread the gospel. While there, his rigid approach to faith began to alienate people. Like that of the Pharisees before him, John's faith had become reliance on following many rules and trying to get others to follow those rules also. Add to this a failed relationship with a young woman who ended up marrying someone else. When John returned to England, he was having a crisis of faith.

> Like each of us, John Wesley experienced rejection.

During this period when he felt like a failure, John attended a religious-society meeting in a house on Aldersgate Street in London. During the meeting, as he was listening to someone talk about faith in Christ, John felt his "heart strangely warmed." This feeling made him realize that although he was following God with his head, he wasn't feeling it in his heart.

John's Aldersgate experience changed the way he viewed faith. It also led him to believe in the importance of grace, the subject of next week's lesson.

Explore Interest Groups

Be sure that adult leaders are waiting when the first child arrives. Greet and welcome the children. Get the children involved in an activity that interests them and introduces the theme for the day's activities.

Never-Ending Bible Verse

- Give each child a half-sheet of paper.

- Have each child fold the paper in half, bringing the long sides together, and then cut the paper along the fold line to make two long paper strips.

- Have each child tape her or his paper strips together to make one even longer strip, taping along the entire edge of the connection point on both sides.

- Encourage each child to bring the ends of the paper strip together but make a half twist in one end just before forming a loop.

- **Say:** You have just made a Möbius (mo-bee-us) strip. A Möbius strip is special because it has no end; it only has one side. You can test this by drawing a line down the center of your Möbius strip. Place your pencil on your Möbius strip and begin drawing a line down the middle. Do not pick your pencil up until you return to the point where your line began.

- Encourage each child to draw a line down the center of the Möbius strip.

- **Say:** Notice that even though you never lifted your pencil, the line is on both sides of the paper. The surface of this Möbius strip is never-ending. God's love for us is also never-ending.

- Show the children today's Bible verse.

- Encourage each child to write the Bible verse on his or her Möbius strip.

- **Ask:** What do you think would happen if we cut our Möbius strip in half?

- Have each child cut along the line drawn on the Möbius strip.

- **Ask:** What happened when you cut your Möbius strip in half? (It became one big circle.)

- **Say:** A circle is a good symbol of God's love for us because it has no end.

Prepare

- ✓ Write the Bible verse ("God's faithful love lasts forever!" Psalm 136:1b) on a markerboard or a piece of mural paper and place it where it can easily be seen.

- ✓ Cut 8 ½-inch by 11-inch paper in half to make 11-inch strips. Each child will need one of these half-sheets.

- ✓ Provide half-sheets of paper, tape, pencils, and scissors.

Things We Can't See

- Show the children one of the balloons.
- **Ask:** What will happen if I blow into this balloon?
- Blow up the balloon and hold it closed with your fingers.
- **Ask:** What is inside the balloon that is making it larger than it was? (Air) Can you see the air inside the balloon? How do you know that the balloon is filled with air?
- Let go of the balloon.
- **Say:** We could not see the air, but we saw the balloon get bigger. And when I let go, we saw the escaping air propel the balloon around the room.
- Blow up the same balloon or another balloon and tie it closed.
- **Ask:** Now that I have tied the balloon so the air won't escape, what will happen to this balloon if I let go of it? (It falls to the ground.) Why does the balloon fall to the ground? (The effect of gravity) Can you see gravity?
- **Say:** We can't see air or gravity, but we can see their effects. God's love is like that, too.
- **Ask:** Can we see God's love? How do you know God loves you?
- Allow children to share their ideas.
- **Say:** When we trust that God loves us even though we can't see God, we call that faith.

Prepare

✓ Provide copies of **Reproducible 3a: John Wesley's Aldersgate Experience**, a puzzle found at the end of this lesson.

✓ Provide pencils.

John Wesley at Aldersgate

- **Say:** Today we are talking about faith. John Wesley was a preacher, but there was a time when he wondered if he should stop preaching. He had doubts about what he should do. During that time, he had an experience that he said was a turning point in his faith.
- Give each child a copy of Reproducible 3a and a pencil.
- Encourage each child to complete the puzzle. (Answer: I felt my heart strangely warmed.)

Large Group

Bring all the children together to experience the Bible story. Use a bell to alert the children to the large-group time.

Where Is John?

- Give each child a copy of the map.

- **Say:** We are continuing to learn about John Wesley. Remember that John lived in England.

- **Ask:** Where was John born? (Epworth)

- Have the children find Epworth on their maps.

- **Ask:** Where did John go to school? (Oxford)

- **Say:** The story we will hear today happens in two different places. John traveled across the ocean to Georgia. At that time Georgia was an English colony.

- Have the children find the state of Georgia on the world map or globe.

- **Say:** When John returned to England, he attended a religious-society meeting at a house on Aldersgate Street in London.

- Encourage the children to find London on their maps.

- Collect the maps to be used next week.

- **Say:** I have hidden a picture of John Wesley and some letters around the room. The letters spell two different things today—*Georgia* and *Aldersgate*.

- Encourage the children to find the picture and letters.

- Have the children work together to put the letters in the correct order to spell *Georgia* and *Aldersgate*.

Faith: Trust in God's Love

- **Ask:** Who have we been learning about? What have we learned about John Wesley so far?

- Encourage the children to review what they have learned.

- Give each child a copy of Reproducible 3b.

- Encourage the children to follow along as you read aloud from the reproducible.

- **Ask:** Why was John discouraged? (He felt that he had failed God while in Georgia.)

- **Say:** For a little while, John forgot that God loves us no matter what and that God is always with us even when we are having trouble. John had his faith restored during the meeting at Aldersgate.

Prepare

- ✓ Use the picture of John Wesley (Reproducible 1b) copied in the first lesson.

- ✓ Provide a copy of the map (Reproducible 1c) for each child.

- ✓ Write each of the following letters on a separate index card: G-E-O-R-G-I-A and A-L-D-E-R-S-G-A-T-E.

- ✓ Have a world map or a globe available.

- ✓ Hide the picture of John Wesley and the index cards around the room.

Prepare

- ✓ Make copies of **Reproducible 3b: Faith: Trust in God's Love**, found at the end of this lesson.

Prepare

✓ If you have not done so, write the Bible verse ("God's faithful love lasts forever!" Psalm 136:1b) on a markerboard or a piece of mural paper and place it where it can easily be seen.

✓ Practice the signs for the Bible verse so you can teach them to the children.

Sign the Bible Verse

- Show the children the Bible verse.

- Encourage the children to read the Bible verse with you.

- **Say:** We are going to learn to say today's Bible verse in sign language.

- Teach the children the following signs from American Sign Language:

  o *God*—Raise your right hand with fingers together and thumb toward you. Begin with the hand raised high as a sign of respect and bring it downward in front of you.
  o *faithful*—Touch the side of your forehead with your right index finger. Then put your right fist on top of your left fist in front of you. Then, keeping your left hand in a fist, put your right hand palm down and brush it over your left fist, moving right to left.
  o *love*—Cross your arms in front of your chest with your fists on your shoulders.
  o *forever*—Point your right index finger upward and make a circle in the air. Then hold your right hand up with the pinky and thumb extended and move your hand away from you.

- Encourage the children to sign and say the Bible verse with you several times.

- **Say:** We have faith that God will never stop loving us.

Worship Time

- **Say:** God loves you and will never stop loving you. Faith is trusting in God's never-ending love. Let's do a cheer for faith.

- Divide the children into six groups. Have each group move to a different area around the room.

- **Say:** Our cheer is going to be, "We have faith, yes we do! We have faith, how about you?" I will choose one group to begin. That group will do a quick huddle to decide which group they will pass the cheer to, then they will say the cheer. When they say "How about you?" they will all point to the group they have chosen. That group will do a quick huddle to decide which group they will pass the cheer to, then they will say the cheer. In this way we will pass the cheer around the room.

- Choose a group to begin the cheer.

- Encourage the children to pass the cheer around the room, making sure every group is included.

- To end the cheer, say, "Last time—this time, everybody answer."

- Dismiss children to their small groups.

Small Groups

Divide the children into small groups. You may organize the groups around age levels or around readers and nonreaders. Keep the groups small, with a maximum of ten children in each group. You may need to have more than one group of each age level.

Young Children (Ages 5-7)

- **Say**: Today we've talked about some things we can't see—air, gravity, faith, and God's love. Even though we can't see God's love, we can feel it—maybe in the hug of a friend or in the love of our parents or when someone smiles at us when we are having a bad day.

- **Ask:** When have you felt God's love?

- Allow children an opportunity to share their ideas.

- **Say:** Faith allows us to trust that God loves us. Today I want you to use your imagination. Imagine what faith would look like if we could see it.

- Give each child crayons and a piece of paper.

- Encourage the children to draw pictures of what they imagine faith might look like. Remind the children that this is their imagination and there is no right or wrong answer.

- Encourage the children to admire each other's artwork.

- **Say:** When you take home this picture that you can see, let it remind you of your faith that you cannot see.

- **Pray:** God, thank you for your never-ending love that we can have faith in. Help us to share your love with everyone we meet. Amen.

Prepare

✓ Provide paper and crayons.

Prepare

✓ Provide Bibles, paper, and pencils.

Older Children (Ages 8–11)

- **Say:** Our Bible verse today is from Psalm 136.

- Have the children find Psalm 136 in their Bibles.

- Encourage the children to read Psalm 136 silently to themselves.

- **Ask:** What do you notice about the end of each verse in Psalm 136? (It's the same.)

- **Say:** This psalm was probably used in worship as a litany. The leader probably read one line and the congregation responded with "God's faithful love lasts forever."

- **Ask:** Look at the lines in the psalm that are not repeated. What are they about? (Things God has done; reasons to praise God)

- **Say:** When we remember things God has done in the past, it reminds us that we can have faith that God will always love us. We are going to write our own litany and use our Bible verse as the response.

- Give each child a piece of paper and a pencil.

- **Say:** Think of a "God sentence" to write on your paper. Write a sentence about God. It could be a description of God or a statement about something God has done for the world or for you personally.

- Have each child write a God sentence on their paper.

- **Say:** We will use our litany as the closing prayer today. We will take turns reading our God sentences. After each person reads her or his sentence we will all respond, "God's faithful love lasts forever."

- Join together in saying the litany the children have written.

John Wesley's Aldersgate Experience

John went to a meeting on Aldersgate Street in London. While he was there, he had an experience that changed his faith. Solve the puzzle to find out what happened.

Identify the missing letter in each row and write it on the line to the right. When you are finished, read down the right-hand column to discover what John said.

A B C D E F G H J K L M N O P Q R S T U V W X Y Z _____

A B C D E G H I J K L M N O P Q R S T U V W X Y Z _____

A B C D F G H I J K L M N O P Q R S T U V W X Y Z _____

A B C D E F G H I J K M N O P Q R S T U V W X Y Z _____

A B C D E F G H I J K L M N O P Q R S U V W X Y Z _____

A B C D E F G H I J K L N O P Q R S T U V W X Y Z _____

A B C D E F G H I J K L M N O P Q R S T U V W X Z _____

A B C D E F G I J K L M N O P Q R S T U V W X Y Z _____

A B C D F G H I J K L M N O P Q R S T U V W X Y Z _____

B C D E F G H I J K L M N O P Q R S T U V W X Y Z _____

A B C D E F G H I J K L M N O P Q S T U V W X Y Z _____

A B C D E F G H I J K L M N O P Q R S U V W X Y Z _____

A B C D E F G H I J K L M N O P Q R T U V W X Y Z _____

A B C D E F G H I J K L M N O P Q R S U V W X Y Z _____

A B C D E F G H I J K L M N O P Q S T U V W X Y Z _____

B C D E F G H I J K L M N O P Q R S T U V W X Y Z _____

A B C D E F G H I J K L M O P Q R S T U V W X Y Z _____

A B C D E F H I J K L M N O P Q R S T U V W X Y Z _____

A B C D F G H I J K L M N O P Q R S T U V W X Y Z _____

A B C D E F G H I J K M N O P Q R S T U V W X Y Z _____

A B C D E F G H I J K L M N O P Q R S T U V W X Z _____

A B C D E F G H I J K L M N O P Q R S T U V X Y Z _____

B C D E F G H I J K L M N O P Q R S T U V W X Y Z _____

A B C D E F G H I J K L M N O P Q S T U V W X Y Z _____

A B C D E F G H I J K L N O P Q R S T U V W X Y Z _____

A B C D F G H I J K L M N O P Q R S T U V W X Y Z _____

A B C E F G H I J K L M N O P Q R S T U V W X Y Z _____

Faith: Trust in God's Love

Faith is trusting and believing in God.

What Does the Bible Say About Faith?

God's love is for everyone. God's love for us will never end.

Faith is trusting in God even though God is not visible.

Have faith even when life is hard. God is still with you.

There are many stories in the Bible about people who had faith in God even when times were hard—people like Abraham, Moses, Noah, Daniel, and many others.

(Based on Romans 5:1-2; Hebrews 11; 2 Corinthians 5:7; and Galatians 3:26.)

John Wesley and Faith

After John Wesley finished college, he worked hard at being a Christian. John wanted everything he did to be for God's glory. John traveled across the ocean to Georgia to share the gospel with the people there. John decided to do this even though it would take more than two months by ship to reach Georgia, and he was terrified of the ocean. On the way to Georgia, John's ship encountered several bad storms. There were times when John was afraid he might die.

John spent two years preaching in Georgia, but his time there did not go well. When John returned to London, he felt as if he had failed God.

In London, John went to a meeting on Aldersgate Street. One of the people at the meeting described how God can work in our hearts through faith in Christ. John later wrote that at that moment, he felt his "heart strangely warmed." John realized that he trusted God. He knew God would always love him and would help him through hard times. John Wesley's Aldersgate experience helped him learn the importance of having faith and trusting in God's love.

4 Grace Accept God's Gift

Objectives

The children will
- hear what the Bible teaches about grace.
- learn about John Wesley's time preaching at Bristol.
- discover that John Wesley preached about grace.
- explore the importance of God's grace.

Theme

Grace is the freely-given gift of God's love.

Bible Verse

You are saved by God's grace because of your faith. This salvation is God's gift. It's not something you possessed. (Ephesians 2:8)

Focus for the Teacher

Grace is an important concept of the Christian faith. Grace is the assurance that God loves us always, no matter what. God loved us even before we were aware of God. There is nothing we need to do or can do to earn grace. God's love is a gift, freely given. Grace is easy to define but may be harder to accept.

Children have to work for grades in school, are reprimanded for behavior that is below expectations, and compete against others to come out as the winner. Teach the children that grace is different. Grace is free. Grace is for everyone. And there is plenty of grace to go around.

Following his experience at Aldersgate, John Wesley became passionate about preaching on the topics of faith and grace. To some, Wesley was obnoxious in his over-the-top enthusiasm, and many churches in London banned him from preaching in their pulpits. This led John to the town of Bristol, where he began preaching outdoors to thousands of people. His message

> There is plenty of grace to go around.

spread and began a movement that eventually became the Methodist church. Wesley wasn't trying to start a new church. He just wanted to share the good news of grace with everyone.

Grace is like that. When we choose to accept God's love for us, we want to share that love with others.

Explore Interest Groups

Be sure that adult leaders are waiting when the first child arrives. Greet and welcome the children. Get the children involved in an activity that interests them and introduces the theme for the day's activities.

Patchwork Grace

- **Say:** Today we are going to make a paper quilt. Each one of you will decorate a quilt square, and then we will put our squares together to make a quilt.

- Give each child a square of paper.

- **Say:** Today we are talking about grace. Grace means that God loves us no matter what. Our quilt will be a grace quilt. Each of you will write the word *grace* somewhere on your quilt square and then decorate your square with whatever designs you choose.

- Encourage each child to write the word *grace* on his or her square.

- Invite each child to decorate the quilt square.

- Let the children arrange the squares on the mural paper.

- Have each child glue his or her square to the mural paper.

- Hang the quilt where others may enjoy it.

Prepare

- ✓ Provide mural paper, six-inch squares of paper, crayons, and glue.

- ✓ Cut a large piece of mural paper to serve as backing for a paper quilt.

- ✓ Lay the mural paper on a table or on the floor.

Grace Notes

- **Ask:** Do you like fun surprises?

- **Say:** Today we're going to make some surprise messages for the rest of the people in our church.

- Have the children cut out a lot of hearts in a variety of sizes from the construction paper.

- Encourage the children to work together and write on each heart "God loves you" or "You are loved."

- When all the hearts have a message on them, have the children distribute the hearts throughout the church where people will find them. You might suggest that they put hearts on some of the seats in the sanctuary or in some of the hymnals. If your church has mailboxes for staff or members, you might put hearts in the mailboxes. Let the children decide where to distribute the hearts (although you may need to declare a few places off-limits).

- **Ask:** How do you think people will feel when they discover a surprise heart? How does it make you feel to leave these surprises?

- **Say:** God's love is for everyone. Thank you for making reminders of God's love.

Prepare

- ✓ Check with your church staff to learn of any places the paper hearts should not go and to be sure the people who clean the church will not clear away the hearts before they are found by other members.

- ✓ Provide construction paper, markers, and scissors

Prepare

✓ Provide a ball of yarn, a roll of tape, and a ruler for each group of four children.

✓ Note: If you have time after the activity, you can challenge the children to spell theme words from the last three weeks: PRAYER, HOLINESS, and FAITH.

Prepare

✓ Provide a copy of John Wesley's picture (Reproducible 1b), along with paper and colored pencils.

✓ Search the Internet or the library for other pictures of John Wesley to show the children.

Spell It

• Divide children into groups of four.

• Have the groups spread out across the room so that each group has a large space on the floor to work in.

• Give each group a ball of yarn, a roll of tape, and a ruler.

• **Say:** I am going to give you a word and then tell you to begin. Your task is to spell the word on the floor with your yarn. You can use tape to hold the yarn in place. Each letter in your word needs to be at least twelve inches high. Your letters can be taller than that, but make sure they are at least twelve inches high. Your word is GRACE.

• Encourage each group to work together to spell the word with their yarn.

• Congratulate each group for completing the task.

• **Say:** Grace is a gift from God. Grace means that God loves us no matter what.

John Wesley Portrait Gallery

• Show the children the pictures of John Wesley.

• **Say:** I want you to imagine that you have been hired to draw a portrait of John Wesley. You can choose whether you want to draw just his head and shoulders or whether you want to draw a picture of him preaching or riding his horse. You are the artist!

• Encourage each child to draw a picture of John Wesley.

• Affirm each child's work.

• Make a John Wesley portrait gallery by displaying the pictures together.

Large Group

Bring all the children together to experience the Bible story. Use a bell to alert the children to the large-group time.

Where Is John?

- Give each child a copy of the map.

- **Say:** We are continuing to learn about John Wesley. Remember that John lived in England. So far we have learned that John was born in Epworth and went to school in Oxford.

- Have the children find Epworth and Oxford on their maps.

- **Say:** Last week we learned about John's trip to Georgia. After he came back from Georgia he spent some time in London.

- Encourage the children to find London on their maps.

- **Say:** When John was preaching in London, not everyone wanted to hear his message. A friend of John's invited him to come to Bristol. That is the story we will hear about John today.

- Have the children find Bristol on their maps.

- Collect the maps to be used next week.

- **Say:** I have again hidden a picture of John Wesley and some letters around the room.

- Encourage the children to find the picture and letters.

- Have the children work together to put the letters in the correct order to spell *Bristol*.

Prepare

✓ Use the picture of John Wesley (Reproducible 1b) copied in the first lesson.

✓ Provide a copy of the map (Reproducible 1c) for each child.

✓ Write each of the following letters on a separate index card: B-R-I-S-T-O-L.

✓ Hide the picture of John Wesley and the index cards around the room.

Grace: Accept God's Gift

- **Say:** Today we are going to hear about John Wesley's time in Bristol and learn what he preached about grace.

- Give each child a copy of Reproducible 4a.

- Invite confident readers to help you read aloud the reproducible.

- **Say:** Think about a time when you messed up, but you were given a second chance. Maybe your parents didn't get as mad as you thought they would when you did something wrong, and they offered you a chance to make things right. Maybe you got to retake a test that you didn't do well on. We all have had times when we received something we didn't really deserve. Grace is like that. We all make mistakes and do things we know we shouldn't do. But God loves us anyway! That's grace!

- **Ask:** Is there anything at all that you can do to make God stop loving you?

- **Say:** No! God loves us no matter what, and there's nothing we can do about it! Isn't that great?

Prepare

✓ Provide copies of **Reproducible 4a: Grace: Accept God's Gift**, found at the end of this lesson.

Prepare

✓ Write this week's Bible verse ("You are saved by God's grace because of your faith. This salvation is God's gift. It's not something you possessed." Ephesians 2:8) on a markerboard or a piece of mural paper and place it where it can easily be seen.

Prepare

✓ Provide mural paper, small pieces of paper, crayons, and glue sticks.

✓ Tape the mural paper on the wall where the children can reach it.

Three-Part Bible Verse

- Show the children the Bible verse.

- Encourage the children to read the Bible verse with you.

- Divide the class into four groups, giving each group a number, 1 through 4.

- **Say:** We are going to divide our verse into three parts. There are three sentences, so each verse will be a part. We'll work together to say the verse. Group 1 will say the first sentence, group 2 will say the second sentence, and group 3 will say the third sentence. Group 4 will then begin again and say the first sentence and then we'll go back to group 1 to say the second sentence. We'll continue in that way until we have said the verse four times and each group has had a chance to begin the verse. You will need to pay attention to know when your group is supposed to talk and what you are supposed to say!

- Encourage the class to say the Bible verse four times as directed.

- **Say:** This verse reminds us that we can't earn grace. It's a gift from God.

Grace Leads to Gratitude

- **Say:** Last week we talked about having faith and trusting that God loves us. Faith allows us to trust in God's grace, to believe that no matter how badly or how many times we mess up, God will still love us and will forgive us for whatever we have done.

- **Ask:** Does that mean we can do whatever we want? (No) Why not?

- **Say:** If we choose to ignore God's grace and do whatever we want, God will still love us. But God wants us to accept grace, and when we do, we realize how amazing God's love for us really is.

- **Ask:** How does it make you feel to know that God loves you no matter what?

- Allow children an opportunity to share their thoughts.

- Give each child a small piece of paper and a crayon.

- **Say:** On your piece of paper, write a message of thanks to God for the gift of grace. Once you have written your message, bring it up and glue it onto the mural paper.

- Encourage each child to write a message of thanks and glue it on the mural paper.

- **Say:** Look at all that gratitude. Accepting God's grace makes us thankful.

- Dismiss children to their small groups.

Small Groups

Divide the children into small groups. You may organize the groups around age levels or around readers and nonreaders. Keep the groups small, with a maximum of ten children in each group. You may need to have more than one group of each age level.

Young Children (Ages 5-7)

- **Say:** Let's review what we've learned today about grace and Wesley.
- Encourage the children to share what they remember.
- **Say:** Today we're going to make a reminder of God's grace.
- Have each child choose two sheets of construction paper.
- Encourage each child to cut a heart shape out of one piece of paper and glue it on the second piece of paper.
- Invite each child to write, "Dear (*child's own name*), I love you. God" on the heart. You may need to help the youngest children.
- Encourage the children to decorate their pictures.
- **Say:** When you're feeling like you've messed up, look at your picture and remember that God still loves you. Always. When we accept God's grace, we want to share it with other people. That means treating others with kindness and love and allowing second chances.
- **Pray:** God of grace, thank you for loving us no matter what. We choose to accept your gift of grace. Help us to pass your love on. Amen.

Prepare

✓ Provide construction paper, crayons, markers, glue sticks, and scissors.

Older Children (Ages 8-11)

- **Say:** Let's review what we've learned today about grace and Wesley.
- Encourage the children to share what they remember.
- **Say:** Today we're going to make a reminder of God's grace.
- Give each child a piece of paper and a pencil.
- Encourage each child to write a letter to herself or himself from God reminding the child of God's love and grace. Let the children know that nobody else will read their letters.
- **Say:** When your letter is finished, you can fold it into a heart.
- Give each child a copy of Reproducible 4b.
- Encourage each child to follow the directions to fold the letter into a heart.
- Invite the children to decorate their hearts.
- **Say:** When you're feeling like you've messed up, read your letter and remember that God still loves you. Always. When we accept God's grace, we want to share it with other people. That means treating others with kindness and love and allowing second chances.
- **Pray:** God of grace, thank you for loving us no matter what. We choose to accept your gift of grace. Help us to pass your love on. Amen.

Prepare

✓ Provide copies of **Reproducible 4b: A Fun Way to Fold a Message**, found at the end of this lesson.

✓ Provide paper, pencils, crayons, and markers.

✓ This activity is fun, but it can be tricky. Be sure to practice folding a heart message before class so that you can help the children with this task.

Grace: Accept God's Gift

Grace is the assurance that God loves us no matter what.

What Does the Bible Say About Grace?

Grace is a gift from God. It cannot be earned.

We have received grace through Jesus.

We are forgiven through grace. Grace is freely given to all.

Grace does not mean we can continue to do things that are not right.

Grace leads to gratitude. When we accept grace we want to live as God wants us to.

(Based on John 1:16-17; 2 Corinthians 4:14-15; Ephesians 1:7; 2:8-10; 2 Timothy 1:9-10.)

John Wesley and Grace

After John's experience at Aldersgate, he preached a lot about faith and grace. Not everyone in London liked John's preaching. Some churches did not want his message and closed their doors to him, not allowing him to preach there anymore.

A friend named George Whitefield invited John to preach in the town of Bristol. John accepted. Lots of people in Bristol made their living in coal mines. Because they were poor, many were not welcomed in churches. For this reason, George had been preaching outside. At first John did not like the thought of preaching outside. But soon John realized he could get his message to many more people that way.

John preached that grace is a gift from God. In other words, God loves us without us doing a thing. We have a choice about whether to accept God's grace. When we choose to accept it, we then want to live as God wants us to and to tell other people about God's gift. John Wesley's message of grace was encouraging to the people in Bristol. The first Methodist church was built in Bristol.

A Fun Way to Fold a Message

1. Lay the piece of paper in front of you with the short edges of the paper at the top and bottom and the writing facing up.

2. Fold the right top corner down so the top edge of the paper is lined up with the left side of the paper. Crease well and then unfold.

3. Fold the left top corner down so the top edge of the paper is lined up with the right side. Crease well and then unfold. Creases should form an X.

4. Fold the top of the paper toward the back, so that the fold runs through the middle of the X you have made. Crease well and then unfold.

5. Hold each side of the paper at the crease you have just made and bring these two points together. Press down the top of the paper so that the upper part of your paper forms a triangle.

6. Fold the bottom corners of the triangle (top layer only) to the top. Then fold the bottom edge of the paper up to meet bottom edge of the triangle. Crease.

7. Fold right and left sides in, bringing them together in the center. Crease well.

8. Turn the paper over. Fold the top point down (top layer only).

9. Fold the bottom right corner up and tuck it into the pocket of the folded-over top point. Crease well. Repeat on the left side.

10. Your paper should have two triangles sticking out of the top. Fold the right triangle down at an angle and tuck it into the same pocket where you inserted the lower right corner.

11. Fold the left top triangle down at an angle. Tuck it into the same pocket where you inserted the lower left corner. Your message should look like a heart!

5 Good Works
Show God's Love and Mercy

Objectives

The children will
- hear what the Bible teaches about good works.
- learn about John Wesley's works of mercy.
- discover that John Wesley preached that faith and good works go together.
- explore ways they can help others.

Theme

Faith and good works go together.

Bible Verse

We are God's accomplishment, created in Christ Jesus to do good things. (Ephesians 2:10a)

Focus for the Teacher

As mentioned previously, the concept of grace was very important to John Wesley, and he preached about it often. Wesley stressed that we are made right with God through grace. No amount of good works can earn God's love. Grace is a gift that cannot be purchased by doing good works.

However, Wesley's belief in grace as a gift did not mean he thought good deeds weren't important. Quite the opposite was true, in fact. Wesley preached many sermons based on the Book of James, stressing that faith and good deeds go together. For Wesley, acceptance of God's grace resulted in gratitude that led to a desire to do good. Wesley encouraged people to do as much good as possible, and he modeled that behavior. While in London, John began a prison ministry. Methodist societies organized the provision of basic medical care and housing to those who were poor. They were also responsible for the formation of many schools for children.

> Grace is a gift that cannot be purchased by doing good works.

Some churches convey the message that the most important aspect of Christianity is a personal relationship with Jesus Christ. Although Wesley would not have argued against it, he probably would have said that focusing only on such a relationship falls short of Jesus' commandment to love God and love our neighbor.

Regarding love of neighbor, it's not enough to have loving feelings; we are to express that love through acts of kindness and mercy.

Explore Interest Groups

Be sure that adult leaders are waiting when the first child arrives. Greet and welcome the children. Get the children involved in an activity that interests them and introduces the theme for the day's activities.

I Can Do Good Things

- **Say:** Today we are going to talk about doing good works. We have many opportunities to do good every day, and I know that all of you do many good things. We are going to play a game about doing good things for other people.

- Choose one child to stand in the center of the circle of chairs. Have the rest of the children sit in the chairs.

- Explain the following rules to the children:

  o The person in the center will say a good thing he or she has done for someone else, such as "I read a book to a younger child" or "I made a get-well card for someone" or "I gave clothes that don't fit me anymore to someone else."
  o Every person in the circle for whom that statement is true must get up and find a new seat, while the person in the middle tries to get a seat also.
  o The person left standing becomes the next person to tell a good thing they have done.

- Encourage the children to play the game.

- **Say:** You have done many good things!

Prepare

✓ Form a circle of chairs facing inward, using one chair fewer than the number of children participating.

Make Thank-You Cards

- **Say:** Today we are talking about doing good works and helping and serving others. We are going to do a service project today. We are going to make thank-you cards for people who serve in our community.

- Let the children know who will receive the cards they make.

- Give each child a piece of construction paper.

- Have each child fold the paper in half, bringing the short sides together, to make a card.

- Have each child place her or his left hand on the back of the card with the thumb and index finger touching the fold.

- Encourage the children to take turns using pencils to trace around each other's hands.

Prepare

✓ Provide construction paper, pencils, scissors, crayons, and markers for the children to make cards.

✓ Decide who will receive the cards. Possibilities include firefighters or police officers in your community, health care workers, and church staff or volunteers.

- Instruct each child to cut out her or his own handprint, beginning at the folded edge and not cutting around the top of the thumb or index finger. The result should be a hand-shaped card that opens up to reveal a cut-out heart shape between the thumb and index finger.

- Invite the children to write thank-you messages on their cards such as "Thank you for your helping hands."

- Encourage the children to decorate their cards.

- Make arrangements for the cards to be delivered.

Prepare

✓ Gather a variety of items useful in ministry, such as a Bible, soup pot, telephone, shovel, coat, offering plate, chalice, musical instrument, adhesive bandage, coffee cup, bread, envelope, crayons, and so forth.

Useful for Doing Good Work

- Show the children all the items you have gathered.

- **Say:** All these items have something in common. Everything here can be used to do God's good work.

- Pick up one item at a time and show it to the children.

- **Ask:** How do you think this item could be used to do God's good work?

- Allow the children to share their ideas about each item. Encourage them to think of many options for each item.

- **Say:** As you can see, there are many different ways to do God's good work.

Prepare

✓ Provide copies of **Reproducible 5a: Faith and Good Works**, a puzzle found at the end of this lesson.

✓ The children will also need Bibles and pencils.

In Other Words

- Give each child a copy of Reproducible 5a, along with a pencil.

- Have each child complete the puzzle. (Answer: You must be doers of the word and not only hearers.)

- **Ask:** What does this mean? How would you say this idea in your own words?

Large Group

Bring all the children together to experience the Bible story. Use a bell to alert the children to the large-group time.

Where Is John?

- Give each child a copy of the map.

- **Say:** We are continuing to learn about John Wesley. Today's story is about a time that John spent in London.

- Have the children find London on their maps.

- **Ask:** What other places on the map have we heard stories about so far? What did John do there?

- Encourage the children to find each place on the map as it is named. Epworth—John was born there. Oxford—John went to school there. Bristol—John and his friend preached near there.

- Collect the maps to be used next week.

- **Say:** I have again hidden a picture of John Wesley and some letters around the room.

- Encourage the children to find the picture and letters.

- Have the children work together to put the letters in the correct order to spell *London.*

Prepare

- ✓ Use the picture of John Wesley (Reproducible 1b) copied in the first lesson.

- ✓ Provide a copy of the map (Reproducible 1c) for each child.

- ✓ Write each of the following letters on a separate index card: L-O-N-D-O-N.

- ✓ Hide the picture of John Wesley and the index cards around the room.

Good Works: Share God's Love

- **Say:** The last two weeks we have learned that faith and grace were important to John Wesley. But John believed there was more to being a Christian than having faith and accepting God's grace.

- Give each child a copy of Reproducible 5b.

- Invite confident readers to help you read aloud the reproducible.

- **Ask:** What did John believe was as important as faith and grace? (Doing good works)

- **Say:** John preached that when we have faith, we want to do good works. He encouraged people to do all the good works they can.

Prepare

- ✓ Provide copies of **Reproducible 5b: Good Works: Share God's Love**, found at the end of this lesson.

Good Works: Show God's Love and Mercy

Prepare

✓ Write the Bible verse ("We are God's accomplishment, created in Christ Jesus to do good things." Ephesians 2:10a) on a markerboard or a piece of mural paper and place it where it can easily be seen.

No Matter How You Say It

- Show the children the Bible verse.

- Encourage the children to read the Bible verse with you.

- **Say:** Now let's say the Bible verse using a soft voice.

- Continue saying the Bible verse together using each of the following types of voices: squeaky, bouncy, fast, slow, loud.

God Is Good All the Time

- **Say:** When I say, "God is good!" you respond, "All the time!"

- Practice this much of the greeting with the children.

- **Say:** When I say, "All the time—" you respond, "God is good!"

- Practice this much of the greeting with the children.

- **Say:** Let's try it all together.

  - o **Leader:** God is good!
  - o **Children:** All the time!
  - o **Leader:** All the time—
  - o **Children:** God is good!

- **Say:** We are going to say a litany together. Listen for your cues.

- Lead the children in the following litany:

  - o **Leader:** We have faith. We trust that God loves us. God is good!
  - o **Children:** All the time!
  - o **Leader:** All the time—
  - o **Children:** God is good!
  - o **Leader:** Grace means that God has always loved us and will never stop loving us. God is good!
  - o **Children:** All the time!
  - o **Leader:** All the time—
  - o **Children:** God is good!
  - o **Leader:** Receiving God's love makes us want to share God's love with others. God is good!
  - o **Children:** All the time!
  - o **Leader:** All the time—
  - o **Children:** God is good!
  - o **Leader:** Amen.

- Dismiss children to their small groups.

Small Groups

Divide the children into small groups. You may organize the groups around age levels or around readers and nonreaders. Keep the groups small, with a maximum of ten children in each group. You may need to have more than one group of each age level.

Young Children (Ages 5-7)

- **Say:** Today we have been talking about good works. Other words we sometimes use for good works are "sharing God's love with others" and "doing service projects." You don't have to be a certain age to share God's love. People of all ages can do good works.

- **Ask:** What are some good works that you can do? What are some ways you can share God's love with others?

- Allow children an opportunity to share their ideas.

- Give each child a piece of construction paper.

- Have each child trace around one hand on the paper, encouraging them to help one another as needed.

- Have each child cut out his or her handprint.

- **Say:** Think of some good works that you can do in the coming week. Write one idea on each finger and on the thumb of your handprint.

- Encourage each child to write ideas of good works on his or her handprint. You may need to help the youngest children with the writing.

- **Say:** Take your handprint home to remind you to do good works this week.

- **Pray:** God, thank you for loving us. Knowing that you love us makes us want to share your love with others. Help us remember to look for chances to do good works. Amen.

Prepare
✓ Provide construction paper, pencils, and scissors.

Prepare

✓ Provide paper and pencils.

Older Children (Ages 8–11)

- **Say:** Today we have been talking about good works. Other ways we sometimes talk about good works include "sharing God's love with others" and "doing service projects." John Wesley encouraged people to do as much good as they can. Let's see if we can come up with one hundred ways to do good.

- Encourage the children to brainstorm ways to do good. Make a list of one hundred ways.

- **Say:** That's a lot of good works!

- Give each child a piece of paper and a pencil.

- **Say:** Look at the list you made and choose five good works that you can do this week. Write them on your paper.

- Encourage each child to choose five good works she or he can do this week.

- **Say:** Take your paper home so that you will remember to do these good works.

- **Pray:** God, we have faith in your love for us. Knowing that you love us makes us want to share your love. Help us always to look for ways to do your good work. Amen.

Faith and Good Works

John Wesley preached that faith and good works go together. Follow the directions below to discover another way to say the same thing.

YOU	WHO	ARE	HEARERS	OF	BIRD
CALLS	MUST	NOT	FAIL	TO	LISTEN
ONLY	THOSE	PEOPLE	THAT	SAY	THE
SECRET	WORD	WILL	BE	ABLE	TO
CALL	EACH	OTHER	THINKERS	AND	DOERS

Use the directions below to find the right words in the grid. Write the words in order on the lines provided. Look up James 1:22 to check your answer.

Begin at the top left corner. _____

Move down 1 space and forward 1 space. _____

Move forward 2 spaces and down 2 spaces. _____

Move down 1 space and forward 2 spaces. _____

Move up 4 spaces and back 1 space. _____

Move down 2 spaces and forward 1 space. _____

Move back 4 spaces and down 1 space. _____

Move down 1 space and forward 3 spaces. _____

Move up 3 spaces and back 2 spaces. _____

Move back 2 spaces and down 1 space. _____

Move up 2 spaces and forward 3 spaces. _____

Good Works: Share God's Love

When we realize how much God loves us, we want to share God's love with other people by doing God's good work.

What Does the Bible Say About Good Works?

God created us to do good works.

Faith and good works go together.

Because God loves us, we want to do good works and share God's love.

Faith and grace cannot be earned by doing good works.

(Based on Ephesians 2:8-10.)

Dear friends, do you think you'll get anywhere in this if you learn all the right words but never do anything? Does merely talking about faith indicate that a person really has it? For instance, you come upon an old friend dressed in rags and half-starved and say, "Good morning, friend! Be clothed in Christ! Be filled with the Holy Spirit!" and walk off without providing so much as a coat or a cup of soup—where does that get you? Isn't it obvious that God-talk without God-acts is outrageous nonsense? (James 2:14-17, *The Message*)

John Wesley and Good Works

John Wesley believed that faith and good works go hand-in-hand, and he stressed that point in his sermons. He encouraged people to do all the good they could. John and his friends lived out this belief in many ways, including ministering to those in prison, providing food and housing for the poor and elderly, and providing education for children. Education was important to John Wesley. The Methodists started many schools, both in England and in America.

6 Perseverance

Stay Awake for God

Objectives

The children will
- hear what the Bible teaches of perseverance.
- learn about John Wesley's final years.
- discover that John Wesley persevered in spite of challenges.
- explore the importance of perseverance in their lives.

Theme

Perseverance means never giving up.

Bible Verse

Stay awake, stand firm in your faith, be brave, be strong.
(1 Corinthians 16:13)

Focus for the Teacher

John Wesley did not intend to start a new denomination. He simply preached what he believed in. He was passionate about his faith and about the gift of God's grace, and he wanted to share that passion with others. Not everyone appreciated Wesley's zeal. His harsh criticism and challenging sermons alienated some people. Wesley wrote in his journals about crowds trying to throw him down the steps or hurl stones at him when he was preaching. People who disagreed with his message even burned down some of the houses where John stayed.

> When people pushed John down he got back up.

This antagonism would have caused many people to give up. But John had learned perseverance from his father, and when people pushed him down he got back up and continued preaching.

John Wesley lived to be eighty-seven, an age that not many people attained in the 1700s. He continued to preach outdoors until the end of his life. Wesley traveled on foot, on horseback, and in a carriage over 250,000 miles around Great Britain. Most often Wesley preached outdoors, averaging fifteen sermons a week—over 40,000 sermons total.

For all the opposition, there were many who welcomed John's message about God's grace. Wesley's faith that engaged the head, heart, and hands appealed to people. In response to his preaching, a revival of Christianity began to take place. The Methodist movement continued to spread and grow, eventually becoming the Methodist church.

Explore Interest Groups

Be sure that adult leaders are waiting when the first child arrives. Greet and welcome the children. Get the children involved in an activity that interests them and introduces the theme for the day's activities.

Perseverance Needed

- Explain the route through the obstacle course to the children.

- Invite the children to take turns going through the obstacle course.

- At random times as each child proceeds through the course, **Say:** Stop! You may not finish the obstacle course now. Go back to the end of the line, please.

- After stopping each child several times, let the children complete the course and cross the finish line.

- **Ask:** How did you feel when I told you that you weren't allowed to cross the finish line? Did you ever want to give up? Why did you keep trying to complete the obstacle course? How did you feel when you were allowed to finish?

- **Say:** Sometimes it's necessary to keep trying even when we keep encountering obstacles and are feeling frustrated. When you keep trying something, it's called perseverance. Perseverance is a good quality to have.

Prepare

- ✓ Create a short obstacle course using objects in the room. For example, you might set up several chairs that the children have to walk around, followed by a couple of hula hoops that have to be stepped in, followed by a table that must be crawled under, and so forth.

- ✓ Place a line of masking tape on the floor several feet in front of the first obstacle and several feet after the last obstacle to indicate the start and the finish line.

Don't Give Up on Finding New Words

- Give each child a piece of paper and a pencil.

- **Say:** Today we are talking about perseverance.

- **Ask:** What is perseverance? (Not giving up)

- Have each child write the word *Perseverance* at the top of his or her paper.

- Encourage each child to find as many new words as he or she can using only the letters in the word *perseverance*.

- Have the children compare their lists.

Prepare

- ✓ Provide paper and pencils.

Prepare

✓ Have on hand a CD player and a CD of upbeat Christian children's music.

✓ Set up a circle of chairs with the chairs facing to the outside of the circle, using one fewer chair than the number of children playing.

Prepare

✓ Provide pencils and copies of **Reproducible 6a: John Wesley Review**, found at the end of this lesson.

Musical Review

- Have the children form a circle around the chairs.

- Start playing music and have the children begin walking around the circle.

- **Say:** When the music stops, find a chair.

- Stop the music and have each child find a seat.

- **Say:** You are not out of the game if you are left standing. Rather, you will tell us something that you remember about John Wesley or the things he preached about.

- Invite the child left standing to share something she or he remembers.

- Remove a chair and start playing the music again, having the children walk around the circle.

- Stop the music and have each child find a seat. This time two people will be left standing.

- Invite each standing child to share something he or she remembers. Encourage them to try to think of things that have not been shared.

- Continue playing, removing one additional chair each round.

John Wesley Review

- **Say:** This is our last week talking about John Wesley. It's a good time to review what we've learned.

- Give each child a copy of Reproducible 6a and a pencil.

- Encourage each child to complete the puzzle. (Key below)

- Ask children to share what they remember about each word.

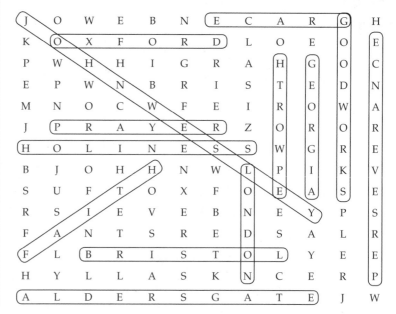

Large Group

Bring all the children together to experience the Bible story. Use a bell to alert the children to the large-group time.

Where Is John?

- Give each child a copy of the map.
- **Say:** Let's review the places we've learned about.
- **Ask:** What places on the map have we heard stories about? What did John do there?
- Encourage the children to find each place on the map as it is named. Epworth—John was born there. Oxford—John went to school there. Bristol—John and his friend preached near there. London—John preached and did ministry there.
- **Say:** I have again hidden a picture of John Wesley and some letters around the room. Today I have hidden the letters to spell all the places we have learned about.
- Encourage the children to find the picture and letters.
- Have the children work together to put the letters in the correct order to spell *Epworth*, *Oxford*, *Bristol*, and *London*.

Prepare

- ✓ Use the picture of John Wesley (Reproducible 1b) copied in the first lesson.
- ✓ Provide a copy of the map (Reproducible 1c) for each child.
- ✓ Write each of the following letters on separate index cards:
    - o E-P-W-O-R-T-H
    - o O-X-F-O-R-D
    - o B-R-I-S-T-O-L
    - o L-O-N-D-O-N
- ✓ Hide the picture of John Wesley and the index cards around the room.

Perseverance: Stay Awake for God

- **Say:** This is our last week learning about John Wesley.
- **Ask:** What have we learned about John Wesley so far?
- Encourage children to review what they have learned.
- Give each child a copy of Reproducible 6b.
- Invite confident readers to help you read aloud the reproducible.
- **Ask:** What obstacles did John Wesley encounter? Do you think he ever felt like giving up? What do you think it means to stay awake for God?
- **Say:** Following God and doing the right thing isn't always easy. We can follow John Wesley's example and never give up.

Prepare

- ✓ Provide copies of **Reproducible 6b: Perseverance: Stay Awake for God**, found at the end of this lesson.

Prepare

✓ Write the Bible verse
("Stay awake, stand
firm in your faith, be
brave, be strong."
1 Corinthians 16:13)
on a markerboard or
a piece of mural paper
and place it where it
can easily be seen.

Wake Up and Say the Bible Verse

- Show the children the Bible verse.

- Encourage the children to read the Bible verse with you.

- **Say:** Since our Bible verse is about staying awake, let's say the Bible verse together while pretending we just woke up.

- Yawn and stretch and read the Bible verse together as a class in a sleepy tone of voice.

What Would John Wesley Say?

- **Say:** We're going to play a game called "What Would John Wesley say?" I am going to make some statements that begin with, "John Wesley would say . . ." If the statement is something that you think John Wesley might have said, jump up and say, "Ding, ding, ding!" If it is not something John Wesley would have said, stay seated and say, "Buzz!"

- Read the following statements, encouraging the children to respond appropriately.

    o John Wesley would say, "My mother and father were not very religious." (Buzz!)
    o John Wesley would say, "I learned the importance of prayer from my mother, Susanna." (Ding, ding, ding!)
    o John Wesley would say, "I once felt my heart strangely warmed." (Ding, ding, ding!)
    o John Wesley would say, "Faith is not important. Doing good works is the only thing that is important." (Buzz!)
    o John Wesley would say, "If you do enough good works you will earn God's love." (Buzz!)
    o John Wesley would say, "Faith and good works are both important." (Ding, ding, ding!)
    o John Wesley would say, "Do all the good you can." (Ding, ding, ding!)
    o John Wesley would say, "God loves you, no matter what!" (Ding, ding, ding!)

- **Say:** I can tell that you have been paying attention and have learned a lot!

- Dismiss children to their small groups.

Small Groups

Divide the children into small groups. You may organize the groups around age levels or around readers and non-readers. Keep the groups small, with a maximum of ten children in each group. You may need to have more than one group of each age level.

Young Children (Ages 5–7)

- **Say:** Since this is the last week of our study on John Wesley, you are going to make a picture that will remind you about what we have discussed.

- Give each child six craft sticks.

- Show the children the lesson themes (prayer, holiness, faith, grace, good works, perseverance).

- Have each child use a marker to write one of the themes on each craft stick. Help the youngest children as needed.

- Give each child a piece of construction paper.

- Encourage the children to glue their craft sticks on the paper in whatever pattern they choose.

- Invite the children to decorate their pictures.

- **Say:** Now you have a reminder of the things we have learned during the last six weeks.

- **Pray:** God, thank you for John Wesley and his teachings. Thank you for your never-ending love for us. Help us to remember to share your love with others in every way we can. Amen.

Prepare

✓ Provide construction paper, craft sticks, markers, and glue sticks.

✓ Write the following words on a piece of paper: *prayer, holiness, faith, grace, good works, perseverance.*

Prepare

✓ Provide construction paper, markers, crayons, pencils, scissors, glue sticks, and yarn.

✓ Provide cans or paper cups to be used as circle patterns.

✓ Write the following words on a piece of paper: *prayer, holiness, faith, grace, good works, perseverance.*

Older Children (Ages 8–11)

- **Say:** Since this is the last week of our study on John Wesley, you are going to make an ornament that will remind you of what we have discussed.

- Have each child use a can or paper cup as a pattern to draw six circles on construction paper. The circles can be different colors but need to be all the same size.

- Have the children cut out their six circles.

- Show the children the lesson themes (prayer, holiness, faith, grace, good works, perseverance).

- Have each child follow these directions to make an ornament:

    o Write each theme on a separate circle.
    o Decorate each circle.
    o Fold each of the six paper circles in half, with the writing facing in.
    o Cut a twelve-inch piece of yarn and set it aside.
    o Put glue on one side of one of the half-circles, covering the complete surface.
    o Attach a different half-circle piece to the first half-circle.
    o Put glue on the unattached half of the second piece.
    o Attach a third half-circle to the second half-circle piece.
    o Glue both ends of the yarn to the half-completed ornament to form a hanging loop.
    o Continue gluing the remaining half-circles in the same manner, gluing the last half-circle to the first half-circle to complete a ball.

- **Say:** Now you have a reminder of the things we have learned during the last six weeks.

- **Pray:** God, we thank you for John Wesley and his teachings. Thank you for your never-ending love. Help us to remember that we can persevere in sharing your love with others because we know you never give up on us. Amen.

John Wesley Review

Find the following words in the word-find puzzle. Words may be printed forward, backward, up, down, or diagonally.

Aldersgate	Good Works	Oxford
Bristol	Grace	Perseverance
Epworth	Holiness	Prayer
Faith	John Wesley	
Georgia	London	

```
J  O  W  E  B  N  E  C  A  R  G  H
K  O  X  F  O  R  D  L  O  E  O  E
P  W  H  H  I  G  R  A  H  G  O  C
E  P  W  N  B  R  I  S  T  E  D  N
M  N  O  C  W  F  E  I  R  O  W  A
J  P  R  A  Y  E  R  Z  O  R  O  R
H  O  L  I  N  E  S  S  W  G  R  E
B  J  O  H  H  N  W  L  P  I  K  V
S  U  F  T  O  X  F  O  E  A  S  E
R  S  I  E  V  E  B  N  E  Y  P  S
F  A  N  T  S  R  E  D  S  A  L  R
F  L  B  R  I  S  T  O  L  Y  E  E
H  Y  L  L  A  S  K  N  C  E  R  P
A  L  D  E  R  S  G  A  T  E  J  W
```

Perseverance: Stay Awake for God

Perseverance is when you keep trying to do something even when it is difficult.

What Does the Bible Say About Perseverance?

The apostle Paul often wrote about perseverance in his letters to churches. During the early days of Christianity, Christians were often persecuted for their faith. It took courage to continue spreading the good news under such conditions. Paul encouraged the early Christians to stay awake in their faith, to stay strong, and to continue spreading the gospel and doing everything in love.

(Based on 1 Corinthians 16:13-14 and Romans 13:11-12.)

John Wesley and Perseverance

At the time when John Wesley lived, many Christians had become lazy. John's preaching challenged his listeners to wake up and to have a deeper faith and a holier life. Many people were inspired by John's sermons, but not everyone was. As John challenged people to change their lives, there were those who opposed his message. Some priests refused to let John preach in their churches. He stopped being invited to preach at Oxford University, where he had gone to school.

John did not give up preaching his message when churches turned him away. Instead, he found new places to preach. John preached outside in fields and in marketplaces. Sometimes the crowd would throw things at John to get him to stop preaching, but John did not give up!

John's perseverance paid off. Many people heard his message of faith and grace and good works. Because of John's persistence and courage, the Methodist church was formed and Christians are still hearing the message today.